The weather was very cold in January. There was snow all over the ground and ice all over the pond.

Kevin and Lotty went to the pond to slide on the ice. Kevin slid along with his legs spread out.

Then Lotty had a turn on the ice. Her legs spread out so much that she went round in a spin.

Wellington went to the pond too.

He tried to tread on the ice,

but he fell head over heels in the

snow.

Then Kevin and Lotty got ready to slide across the ice together. 'Ready, steady, go,' barked Wellington.

Kevin and Lotty slid along the ice. Oh no! The ice cracked. Kevin fell in the water. His head went under the ice.

SPLASH! Lotty fell in after him. The two dogs went under the water. They came up for a breath.

They tried to get back on the ice, but their heads kept going under the freezing water.

Wellington jumped on the ice with a heavy thud. He cracked it too. He was strong. He swam to meet Kevin and Lotty.

He rescued them from the freezing water. They were very cold but glad to be alive. They did not tread on icy ponds again.

'ea'

head   spread
tread   ready
steady   heavy
breath   weather

soft 'c'

ice   icy

Other Vocabulary:

Phase 2: in on and his legs a up at of fell him dogs get back but got did not had

Phase 3: Kevin with much that thud them along then

Phase 4: pond went slid spin splash kept strong swam glad across from

Vowel Digraphs:

ay/ai/: again (came)
ee/ea: meet heels freezing
oa/ow: snow (cold)
oo: too (rescued)
ou/ow: out ground round
ar: barked
or: for
er: over water under after together
ie/i-e: tried alive slide

Tricky words:

the was very there all to have go her oh no he she they their going be two so

Other words:

turn January cracked came Lotty Wellington jumped